TO DAD

with love
Victoria and Henrietta
Christmas 1979

A gift book
written by children
for fathers everywhere
Edited by
Richard & Helen Exley

Published by Exley Publications Ltd.

By the same editors

The Missionary Myth, 1973
Grandmas and Grandpas, 1975
To Mum, 1976
What is a Husband? 1977
Happy Families, 1977
Cats (and other crazy cuddlies), 1978
Dogs (and other funny furries), 1978
Dear World, 1978

Alison Wheeler A

To Lincoln and Dalton

©EXLEY PUBLICATIONS, 63 Kingsfield Road,
Watford, Herts.

First printing September 1976
Second printing November 1976.
Third printing October 1977
Fourth printing February 1978
Fifth printing August 1978

Front cover drawing by Richard Wakeford, age 7.
Back cover drawing by Timothy Darwell-Smith, age 7.

Printed in Great Britain by Morrison & Gibb Ltd, Edinburgh.

ISBN 0 905521 01 3

2

When my dad comes in from work the house fills with laughter.

Thomas Telford Age 11

Dads are funnier than mums, we think. Especially after reading what children have to say about them. The love is as strong — that shows even in the funniest entries. But dads are such fun to be with and love being laughed at and laughed with.

We had nearly 5,000 entries for this book, and the companion volume TO MUM, sent in by schoolchildren from all over the world. The entries were about dads quietly going into the fields two hours before breakfast. They were about other dads dashing off to a computer world. They were about working dads and thinking dads. But most of all they were about kind, playful dads who, no matter how worried or busy, always had time for a lesson in life or just a tickle. These much praised dads came from Britain, the United States, India, Australia, New Zealand, Trinidad, Jamaica, Denmark, Eire, France, Germany, Holland, Italy, Spain, Switzerland, Cyprus, Egypt, Israel, Turkey, Saudi Arabia, South Africa and Nigeria. We are deeply grateful to the dozens of schools that helped in the compilation of the book, and to all the children who made the job so enjoyable.

We've left the spelling just as it came to us, except where the meaning went squiff. We haven't even been too fussy about which entries finally made it, because sometimes ten children said almost the same thing about their dads. We hope that all those children whose entries were not chosen, will feel that someone else has said what they wanted to say.

So to you, a universal dad, comes this 'thank you' from children everywhere. And if the book comes to you as a gift from your own child, we're sure he or she would have liked to have said some of these things — if they haven't been said already!

Richard & Helen Exley

What is a dad?

Dads are people whom you can call nick names with out getting thumped.

Peter Smith Age 9

Dads are the kind of people that say "Money does not grow on trees", and "It's too early to think of Christmas".
They sometimes play a game with you but mostly sit in their study working out problems.

James Donaldson Age 10

The proverbial dad with a slipper waiting for you to do something wrong, died out years ago. Nowadays dads are not like that. They are strict but are nice people.

Trevor Burgess Age 12

In the crazy world of television, people seem to think that dads are funny things that live in paint-pots and jump up and down on the best dining-room table singing about Birdseye Supermouse. In fact they are not. They are really perfectly sane things that would spank you if you tried to do the same.

Guy Hannaford

Dads should be treated with respect because they put up with us.

Allan Wotherspoon Age 12

Fathers are people whom you have to have but you sometimes wish were not there.

Andrew

A father is someone who tries to teach you to play football even though you are a girl.

Jane Moppel Age 12

Mums wear dresses to cuver theer knickers and bras. Dads wear long pants to cuver theer underpants.

Timothy

4

A dad is a man mum but unlike a mum he is not always on the telephone.

Clare Dawkins

A dad is a lion—king of the jungle;
A dad is a mouse—often attacked by a cat,
commonly known as a mum;
A dad is a fox—hunting his helpless, innocent
victim—his son;
A dad is a lamb—he shies out of family society;
A dad is a dog—not a man's best friend—the
one who barks out orders;
A dad is a gannet—a devourer of food, beyond all
rations;
A dad is a guinea-pig—the fool who dares sample
his angelic daughter's cooking;
A dad is a goat, a scapegoat—regularly forced
by his children to shoulder any blame;
A dad is a flea—the first to flee when mother-in-law
arrives!
A dad is a donkey—the simple one who bears the
burdens of others;
A dad is a sparrow—so common!
A dad is . . . a human?

Jeremy Age 14

Fathers like to think they are responsible, dutiful, orderly and keen, and they endeavour to convince their children of this.

Julia Age 12

A father's shoulder is something to sit upon when there is a crowd and you can't see.

Jacqueline Small

Dads are people who can sleep anywhere. Dad always asks how you got on at school. Dad never likes to be disturbed in the midle of the news.

Chris Age 9

Father's all way's get grey hair before mother's.

Steven Age 10

Most dads never clear up after themselves.

Louise Age 10

Dads usually carry a slipper for naughty boys like my friend.

Simon Age 9

A father is someone who has alful toe nails.

Lois Age 11

A dad is a man who tries to look very handsome to get a lady so they can get married and also have children.

Brenda Newnan Age 12

A father is a person who lets you do things your not spos to do.

Simon Cargill Age 11

A dad is a person who is tucked behind the newspapers every Sunday.

Wendy

A father all ways starts a fight and then when we start to fight him he all ways get's cross but not for long because we start tiggling him.

Steven Age 10

Dad is the one that wallops me.

Simon Age 10

Dad

Darren
Eaton
age 9

My dad watches Kojak and Cannon because they are more bald and fat than he is.

Mark Wickham-Jones Age 13

Bilge Age 13

Baldy

Fathers are sometimes thin on top and some are as borld as a babies bottom.

Dave Clark Age 14

Because my dad is so bald, he says his hair slipped down onto his chin to make a beard.

Mark Age 13

My dad's bald, if he wasn't he wouldn't be half as lovable.

K Hosford Age 15

Thomas Age 8

All shapes and sizes

Dads wear socks so that We can not see there hairre legs.

Sara Beesley

Dad's wear wig's to hide there tatty hair.

Sean Age 8

My dad often wears a tatty green cardigan with holes in the elbows. He says that these holes are there so that his elbows can breathe.

Rebecca Skett Age 11

My father likes comfortable clothes, like old corduroys and towling shirts, they look a bit messy though, so we have to dress him up in respectable clothes.

Emma Age 10

My dad is tall and large out ways. His eyes are popping out but when he is happy they go back in his head.

Helen Francis Age 7

My dad is nearly six foot three. He's lot more bigger than you.

David Burkey

Karen Murray Age 10

Neil King Age 9

David Royffe

Some are big and strong,
Some are small and fat
Some are thin and some are thick
What funny dads we've got!

Janice Jones

My dad is a bit bald,
My dad is fat,
My dad isn't old
Well not quite yet.

Jane Age 11

Dad has got a sweet tooth,
And I mean a sweet *tooth*
He's had all the rest out!

Lisa Age 10

Paul Lowe Age 7

Christopher Pearson Age 8

Victoria

Brigitte Corbett Age 6

11

Behind the wheel

Dads drive too fast and get Summuneds.

John Age 12

Fathers always take very good care of their shiny cars, and seem to think that their wives will scratch them.

Emma Age 10

Dads think that they are the greatest drivers in this world. They usually comment on mums' driving. Usually the mums are right because they are naturally cautious and men have to show off. Please do not get the idea that I am a supporter of Women's Liberation, nothing could be further from the truth. Anyway when I drive I will always be right.

Ovenden

My father finds faults about my mother's driving constantly. Go left, go right, your driving is too fast and too slow. But when he is driving he does the same things himself.

Farhad Age 8

Money reminds me of Dad because He is an accountant at Tuckton park. Paint reminds me of Daddy because he is decrating the house. If I sea a crash It reminds me of Daddy driving The car.

Timothy Age 9

Dalton Age 9

Off to the pub

If my dad sees a "Do you smoke?" sign he proudly announces 'No I have never smoked' to which I reply 'It's just as well the amount you drink'.

David

Every night my dad goes to the pub for a pint of beer and my mum gets quite angry. The car he's got is a Renault 12 and the colour is lightish blue. I think his hobbie is driving and drinking.

Sandra Age 11

A dad is someone who goes to the pub a lot. While they are there they drink and play dominos and darts. Sometimes they come home drunk singing lullabies.

Mark

A father is a person who drinks about four pints of beer, and next day has a headake.

Mark Age 10

Stuart

Poor old Dad...

Dads are very good at working in the garage and mucking the house up.

Joanne Age 11

If anything is out of place, you know that Dad is here. If you think something's fool proof, you do not know my dad.

Lisa Age 10

I am sorry not to be on familiar terms with my dad but our ideas don't agree: his are out of date!

Rosalba Age 14

Dad's the sort of man who trys to work out problems but takes a jolly long time about it.

Jane

My dad usually knows where to go on Sunday, but only the day after!

Marilena Age 14

Dad is the person who goes out to fix the car, but in the end it has to be taken to a garage.

Peter

My absent-minded father often calls me by my auntie's name and asks me to hurry up and polish my clothes and iron my shoes.
Whenever I ask him whether I could go for a tour, camp or picnic, he immediately says 'no', and I am happy, for then I am sure of going. But once when he spontaneously said 'Yes' I was put into a great confusion.

Poorna Age 15

One of my dad's main pleasures in his cricket. He plays in a local village team all through the summer. He has the most stylish miss I've ever seen.

David

Dad is old
Dad is wise
He keeps his learning in disguise.
I am getting more and more learned than dad
Because he did not do parabolic graphs when he was a
lad.
Simon Age 10

I really don't know why
Dad thinks he knows everything
But when you ask him 7 × 7
He says 56! daft old dad.
Vanessa Age 10

My dad tries to play golf,
Trys to ski,
Trys to play rugby,
But so far he just hasn't been lucky.
Philip Age 12

My dad is strong.
He's always up to things he is.
He hammers his fum,
Once he hammed his fum
And he had to go to hostpital he did.
Karen Age 8

Dad gets your french homework wrong.
Dad sleeps in his armchair all Sunday.
Dad is someone who trys to explain how the
kitchen shelf fell down.
Dad fixes the car and then has to send it
to the garage to be mended.
Dad had to walk five miles to school
when he was a lad.
Dad was almost picked for England.
Dad is always talking about how he's going
to have Solar Pannels installed.
David

Theodore Thomas

15

The boss

My dad thinks his the boss. So do I. It's not Fair my dad gets the biggest dinner and Pudding my dad likes it.
My dad Throws his smelly soucks at me.

Michelle Age 10

I like Dads becase he rules the television and he rules it well.

Rowan Ellis Age 7

Fathers are usually very strict and expect one to jump when spoken to.

Kevin Age 12

Dads are. people to respect and obey. Whatever they say must be firstly not disobeyed and secondly respected and done with as much enthusiasm as if you wanted to disobey.

Christopher Hollingshurst Age 12

If it was not for my father there would be no discipline and it would be very boring.

Tony Martin Age 12

Fathers all like listening to the family radio, and most of them like reading. If their wife wants to read they usually get impatint, but if they want to read their wife isn't allowed to be impatint.

Margaret Age 10

My dad is qwit strict,
He gets cross because he is tired and fed up.

John Age 9

Fathers should all be a little strict and not all spoilers of children. Fathers are in theory the owners of the house, the car and the bikes. Most fathers are more severe than mothers although they are liked equally well.

Susan Abbott Age 10

When anything goes wrong, Dad is completely unbiased and blames me.

Michael Haworth-Maden Age 12

Thomas Age 8

Daddy Age 44

Lazybones

A dad is someone who says he will do something some time, but the time never comes.

John

My dad has a funny hobby which I think is being lazy.

James Age 8

My daddy is lazy Because He always sits on his bottom.

Billie Age 6

Dads are never working unless they are forced to by mums.

David Age 12

My dad believes in everybody doing their fair share. So that when we go into the lounge after cutting the grass, we see him lying on the sofa and watching T.V.

Julie Age 11

When my mummy goes out my dad has to go to his mummy and have dinner.

Jason Age 9

A dad is someone who will finish making a cupboard in the year 2000!

Joyce Blair

Some typical dad's talk:
'I'll mend the door tomorrow.'
'But the ironmonger's shut.'
'But the ladder is broken.'

Genevieve   *Orsini Age 13*

Michael
Hellicar
Age 8

In praise of dads

In my opinion a father is a 'VIP' in his family!

Laura Antonucci Age 11

My father is really peaceful: if the world fell down he wouldn't be surprised!

Lorena Checconi Age 11

What I like best about my dad is that he is proud of me when I do well in class, and even when I get low marks he is still proud of me. I love him for that.

Anjanee Bissessarsingh Age 10

If I didn't have Pa I think the world would be black.
He always help me with mi multiplications.

Darrell James Age 11

Dads love you more than anyone.

Claire Powell Age 9

Father

Somebody that I
Can come to when
I'm sick
Worried
Wrong
Somebody that
Can tell me the
Solution
To life
AND
Progress;
And give me
HOPE
To go on.

Helen Holm Age 10

*Ali Abbas
Hanif Age 8*

Thank Heaven for dads

Dads usually ask you if you have had a nice day at school or wherever you have been. They are very busy people but they are never too busy to give you a kiss.

Katharine Rule Age 9

Thank heavens someone invented dads.

C Matthews

My father sometimes cooks a lovely chicken dinner. My dad tells me that he loves me very much. Dad made the family a fish pond. My dad is a carpenter. Dad makes all our cupboards. Dad made me a dollshouse and Dad is very kind to me. Dad buys me sweets everyday and I love Dad very much.

Barbara Webb Age 9

I like my father because he is always ready to listen and help me out of my troubles, big or small. He takes care of me and treats me well. He does not hesitate to give me something when I ask him for it. My father helps me when I am doing something difficult, and I always feel safe and sound when he is around. Sometimes, when I get him angry he will frown and I will pout, but soon afterwards he's his own self again. I think my daddy is my best friend, even when I am in difficulties, and I like him very much.

Maltie Maraj Age 11

My father is very funny and very pleasant. When he comes back home from work and is very tired, he cheers up as soon as he sees us.

Nadia Caraccio Age 12

But seriously, I think dads are one of the most important assets a child can have. Don't you?

A McAuilhin

Good old Dad. He is adorable.

Antigoni Kalodiki Age 14

Katy Low

I want the whole world to know my dad is very nice and kind to me.

Sharon Chapler Age 10

Life's truths

Who let me help him fix a car tyre?
Who showed me love when I grew up?
Who told me the straight way to go?
Who smoothed the slippery way for me?
This tribute goes to my father

Michelle Ellery Age 13

My dad has taught me to think, before I go to bed, over what progress I've made during the day. He always encourages us to read more books, increase our knowledge and vocabulary and enrich our language. His favourite motto is 'Service before self' and he has taught me: 'First deserve and then desire.'

Amitabh R. Shah

When I don't go to school in the afternoon and my father is free from work, we talk a lot. Even when he is very tired he is ready to listen to my problems and he always knows how to advise me.

Barbara Frasca Age 11

Mark Farrell

The breadwinner

A dad is One of the most Important people in a family because he earns money to keep the whole family living. So that means that a father is some-one who Cares for you. A father is a thing that you depend on.

Simon M Leese

A dad is a man who goes to work. And works all day long. And looks forward to coming home and seeing his family. He works hard all day so he can earn a lot of money to bring back to his family so he can pay the taxes and to pay for all the things a family needs.

Amanda Wilcock Age 8

After his breakfast away he goes to do what he needs to do for us. Don't know what he does, but in the evening, when he gets home his face is tired. Sometimes he comes home at lunch, and the talk is full of his meetings with strange people about strange things. The need for money, and those who suffer from the government. Land being taken over, or rents not paid.
This happens for the full week, but in the week-end he is different. Same bright eyes in a bright face, his black hair shining in the sun. He goes away to sail, one of his joys, and spends a day with friends and exercise. He is always changed after a break. Despite his office work, he is one who will always be with you.

Douglas Age 12

A dad is the person in the house who has a lot of money. He looks after the water and electricity bills and answers the important letters and pays school and milk fees. He buys new cars and he bought the house for us.

Timothy Butcher Age 8

ire Cummins Age 10

Julie Bonser
Age 9

BOB

Arielle Griffiths Age 8

Francis Price Age 9

Dads are lads who work all day,
They keep their family on their pay;
They come both small,
They come both tall;
And they're helpful and kind in every way,
Doing their work day by day.

Guy Miller Age 8

Denise Howie Age 14

Life without them

I feel sorry for all the orphans all over the country without dads to look after them.

Brian Whitney

I don't know what I would do without my dad I would not have any Cristmas presents No birthday presents No food no shelter No were to live No nothing.

John Seane Age 9

We're lucky to have a dad. With no dad we would have no food, no home. If people had no children England would have no people, no King, no Queen.

James Lewis

I think really dads are a nuisance but you can't do with out them!

Paul

David Fraser

Sarah Galant

Carol
Greenw
Age

A very happy moth
A very happy fath
is what A family
should be like.

Tracy Hampton
Age 6

Dad is away

Mum goes quietly up to bed,
I start to think of the tears she might shed.
Dad has gone and we're alone,
To live in this house of cold stone.
And he won't be back for another six months.

Dad is away on business,
The house is in a complete mess.
Mum does not seem to care,
About the house or what she'll wear.
She is very pretty my mum is,
But she looks untidy by wearing shirts that are his.
I wish she would tidy herself up.

Dad is coming home tomorrow,
Now there will be no more sorrow.
It's nice to see mum happy again,
I can see a tremendous change.
It's great having him home.

Angela Age 15

James Beasley
Age 7

Big, strong and kind

Fathers are big and strong and kind.

Aine Hunt Age 11

D-A-D-D-Y, D-A-D-D-Y. Every child needs a lot of love, attention and to know someone cares for them no matter what.

J Stevens Age 14

Dad helps me through my doubts and fears.

Ruth James Age 11

A father is the first person to help a child during difficulties. Just as an old man's main support is his stick, a child's main support are his father and mother.

Sandeep Sampat Age 15

A father is someone who when he comes home from work and is tired still listenes to you talking. A father is someone who understands you.

Lois Looering Age 11

Dads are the ones who when Mother's Day comes round buys a present and says its from you.

A McAuilhin

A father is the backbone of a family.

Paul Marshall Age 12

James Age 6

I always feel safe with Dad.

Anne Fowka Age 11

32

Peter Fey Age 10

What are dads for?

Dads are for pocket money, being boss, gardening, fishing, shooting, and any other pleasures that they can think of; that includes sleeping under a newspaper and pretending to be reading it.

Deborah Age 13

In the home a dad is very important. He is the person who provides us with money to feed and clothe ourselves. He can decorate your bedroom, mend your radio, makes cages for your pets, repair a puncture in your bicycle tyre and help you with your maths homework. A dad can be very useful for taking you in the car to and from parties, music lessons, and dancing lessons. A dad is the person whom you ask for pocket money. He is the one who complains about the time you spend talking on the telephone, as he has to pay the bills. A dad is someone who will support you in an argument, if he believes you to be right. He is someone who reads your school report, and treats you if it is good. A dad likes to come into a nice happy home in the evening, and settle back in his chair with a newspaper. He likes to recall his National Service days. On your wedding day he is again very useful, as he is needed to walk up the aisle and give you away. Although dads do not show it, they worry about you an awful lot.

Beverley Wilkins Age 13

Charlotte Hansen
Age 8

A father is for staying home to be with his son.

Robert McConchie Age 12

Dads are helpful, but in another way,
They are not there to do your hair
But to undo sticky problems.
That's why Dads are there.

Sarah Edworthy Age 11

A dad is:
Someone to read you a bedtime story
Someone to have a fight with
Someone to burn the toast
Someone to go out to the pub.

Sara Age 9

Dalton Exley

My Dad's working and keeps the house going. He tells you things that make you laugh. He buys you things for Christmas. He takes you for rides in the countryside so you should think kind things. He smacks you and teaches you and puts you to bed.

Darren Age 9

Fathers are for erning money and helping to keep the human race going.

Susan Abbott Age 10

35

Being with Dad

Now dad, he is the nice sort,
He'll sit and watch TV
And sheer bliss are the evenings
When I'm sitting on his knee.

Susan Harvie·Age 10

As a small child, I will always remember our family sitting beside a roaring fire in the lounge, intent on our father as he read to us, the curtains shutting out the black night.

Elisabeth Cowey Age 13

A father is a person who you love very much. He is never tired of hearing your jokes.

Eduardo Vivo Age 8

My house is lonely when my father is at work.

Clara Ortega Age 8

I like my daddy.

Richard de Cesare

Ferhan Kurtulmus Age 9

Kung fu dads

I like my dad because he fights me.

Darren P Griffin Age 7

My dad holds me by the middle, and says one, two, three. He pretends that he is going to throw me out of the window, but he realy throws me on to my bed. My dad runs up stairs pretending to be a monster.

Nicola Jane Hickson Age 8

When dad me wakes up I usually burrow under the covers, because he turns on his radio and puts it on my ear. Then he tickles my feet when I turn upside-down.

Charles Dornton Age 11

I like my dad when I have a fight with him. If he does not I call him an old man and he starts to chase me around the house and garden.

Stuart Hughes Age 9

My dad is the kind of person that does Kung Fu on me and pulls me out of bed with a Kratie chop. Every holiday he gets my big brother to teach me how to kick my dad back.

Andrew Pinder Age 10

Fathers are people that will fight with you but not hurt you.

Christine Johnston Age 11

Harold Age 9

Saturday morning

The thing I like about my dad is he is very cuddly and soft especially on Saturday morning. I always creep in and snuggle up to him.

Suzanne Pinder Age 12

On Saturday morning Mummy is marvellous. Out of bed she jumps (well, not exactly jumps) but she gets out of bed and down to the kitchen she goes tiptoeing, where she begins her wonders, bacon and eggs, sausages and tomatoes, kidneys (on special treats) toast and a super cup of coffee for breakfast nothing burnt (usually).
Meanwhile Daddy is still fast asleep, but as usual his bliss is ended by the four of us jumping on his bed waiting for one of his super stories. I find that Daddy's stories are marvellous, they are exciting, frightening, amusing but above all imaginative. He is very good at those stories (Daddy made) but he always stops when there is a slight hint of breakfast, I wonder why? Daddy (I suppose) is patient, strong-hearted and above all super. He protects all of us like a shepherd guarding his sheep (he even bleats, that is snores). He is tall, dark and handsome and though he is not fat he eats quite a bit. Mummy never eats anything (she saves it all for Daddy) which he likes.
I don't know where I'd be if my dearest mother and father weren't by my side.

Belinda Scarborough Age 12

Graham Weiss

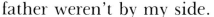

Just a big kid?

When I get my train set out, my dad takes over the controls, and I have to work the points. But my dad does have some good points, he lets me take over the controls sometimes about 5 minutes before bed time.

Nigel Age 10

Dad's know what it is like to be a kid and they know what we will be up to like knicking gates and knocking on doors.

Dave Age 14

My dad is very good at Monopoly. He makes the rules up as he goes along.

Fraser Age 11

When Leeds win a match he leaps up in the air, screeching "Yippee!" or "Yahooh!" or "Yahay!"

Sophia Davies Age 11

Jesper Vaver Age 9

My dad is a big kid because he always wants to read my Beanos.

Carl Age 8

Witney King

Fun and games

My daddy lays on the floor and me and my sister get on him. We pretend he is a donkey.

Susan Lamb Age 5

My dad is brilliant but lazy too because he always stays in bed when I am up. I like it when Dad lays on the floor because when he is not watching I sit on his tummy and start thumping him but he says it does not hurt him.

Amber Macdonald Age 10

William Brown Age 10

A dad plays with you and pretends to fight you.
A dad gives you your pocket money.
A dad helps you make things.
My dad plays with my soldiers.
My dad takes us out.
Dad takes the corks off bottles.
Dad buys my christmas presents.
Dad takes us sailing.
Dad takes me shopping on holiday and at the weekends.
Dad teaches me to do new things like sums.
Dad is very nice to me.

Neil Wilson Age 8

A dad is someone who on the only day he doesn't work takes you swimming.

Elisabeth Fenton Age 12

Andrew Green

Dads have hairy legs and big knee caps. Dads play with you and put you on their backs and toss you off and play tick with you.

David Owen

In the snow dads always pull you along on the sled, and they put up a good snowball fight. If you go out with your dad you can guarantee that you have a good time. Dads always seem to make things fun.

K Abele

Father can be a playful fellow. He'll tell the little children in the house a joke or two to make them jolly, to make them happy, merry children instead of miserable grumpy ones. That's what I like.

Jemima Age 7

My dad

My daddy is a headmaster. My daddy likes Rugby and Football. Daddy is clever and strong, hairy, cuddly and small.

Liam Age 7

On Sunday morning my dad preaches at church and I never feel he is too good to be true.

Sally Age 11

My wonderful, loving, generous, thoughtful, clever, patient dad is in possession of all the qualities I have just listed.

Timothy Scott Norris Age 12

My daddy is a round table and he sets off fire works.

David Beniston Age 7

My dad is realey quite a tidy man for a Hells Angel.

Christopher Age 12

Jeremy Solomon

My dad reminds me of an oak tree. He's big, solid, old, untidy and rather splendid.

David

Luengo

The things children say

One day my dad got married to a lady, her name was Elaine. Then they went on a honeymoon and they had a baby boy. His name is Brian but they had another baby, when they came home. It was a little baby girl. Its name was Sherry. After a coulpe of weeks my mum had me and she named me Rebecca.

Rebecca Age 9

I found out about Father Christmas when Dad dropped all our toys on the wooden floor outside my bedroom and from then on I knew why my Mum always put beer out for Santa, not milk.

Andrew Simpson Age 12

But one thing is my dad will not hit my mam he says if a man hits a woman he is a bit bent. We say he won't hit my mum as she can hit harder than him.

Christopher Age 14

My daddy has naughty habbits they are, Daddy says that Mommy has got is Keys but Mommy says she hasn't and Daddy says she has so Mommy says Look in your pocket so Daddy looks in his pocket and all that time he had them in his pocket.

Tracey Age 8

My dad has a habit of buying my mum chocolates and eating them himself.

Craig Cohen Age 9

My father is Welsh and has the terrible habit of singing ear-splitting Welsh hymns at the table.

Gareth Age 10

Tina Vowles Age 5

Joanne Rudge

My mother likes to have babies, but my father doesn't like to have babies.

Paul Age 8

My daddy is funy He has false teeth and wen He gos to Bed He puts them under the Bed and wen my mummy gos to Bed my daddy false teeth Bits my mummy and she jumps out of the Bed.

Mary Age 7

New dads always take on a smug self-satisfied expression of haven't-we-done-well, and they love having their little Achievement admired. But once the little achievement learns how to a) bawl incessantly b) ask for money and pull tablecloths from tables — 'like the man did on telly' — their faces change to an expression of why-did-we-bother.

Lorraine Phelps

When I'm a Dad

On Saturdays I'd take them to the football match (Utd. will be playing) or to the pictures. The kids will not support any other football team but Manchester United and Glasgow Celtic. If they support a rubbish team like Leeds Utd. they will not get any presents for their birthday or Christmas.

I Dearnaley Age 13

Dads should not be bothered by little pests or tugged and pulled to come and play football. Parents should be treated nicely.

Gregory Hassall Age 8

Daniel Chua
Age 9

48

Holding forth...

Dads of today seem to spend most of their waking moments telling their unfortunate offspring how much harder life was in their day and yet never waste a moment in saying what a state the country's in and start reminiscing about the Good Old Days.

Julia

'Waste Not, Want Not' is a phrase that continually escapes from Dad's lips, seconded only by 'When-I-was-your-age-I didn't-have-as-much-as-you-do-now' and 'Kids!'

Lorraine

Every person needs a dad
But sometimes they are a bore,
When Dad is saying
What he did in the war.

Geraint Age 12

Fathers are always right, and even if they're not right, they're never actually wrong.

Catherine Age 12

Sarah Gammen

My dad is always making up stories of how he killed a lion in Africa, or how he used to jump out of his window and go for a swim down the Thames. One day he told me that when people wore drainpipe trousers, they unscrewed their feet to put them on. Sometimes Mum gets fed up with him.

Jane Age 13

I never ask my father questions because he is so clever that he goes into details I do not understand.

Mark Wickham-Jones Age 13

Whenever I am watching a film, my father comments on it all the time saying 'That's silly! He can't kill someone that far away with a hand pistol.' All through the film he makes comments like that. It becomes very annoying, after all, if he is so good at making films, why doesn't he become a film producer?

Sarah

A dad is always watching football, muttering on that he could do better when he was a kid.

Julia

My dad can just talk and talk with nobody listening.

Peter Age 10

Cassidy Age 7

On the war-path

When dads lose their temper, They go red, then purple, then red again.

Paula Age 11

Dad sometimes has bad days, so we try to be good and quiet.

Sally Age 11

When Mum's in a temper you're shouted at. But when Dad's in a temper you're for it.

Simon Age 11

When my dad is in a bad mood it isn't the most pleasant ordeal for who he's in a bad mood with.

David Age 11

When my dad gets very mad he kicks the central heating.
When my dad's in a good mood he goes to the pub.

Alex Age 11

He's the good shepherd watching o'er you now, though when he smacks you its "Ow, ow, ow."

Sally Age 13

My dad says that sometimes I'm very bad. But I bet that my dad was *always* bad when he was small.

Celia Age 9

Dads grow big hands to spank people.

Scott

A resistance army?

In my mind dads can be likened to a big army that has it's curfews, short hair, training and general discipline. The kids can be likened to the resistance army with it's long hair, no set curfews, rebellion to the ruling army's dictatorship, no cultural training, no discipline and very positive attitudes when it comes to putting spokes in the wheels of the ruling army.

Peter Visser Age 15

Sometimes fathers are strict about table manners, which I think is rotten because you can't have a meal without, "Blow your nose!" or "Keep your mouth closed!" when you eat! When you find a packet of biscuits after a good rummage in the food cupboard, they take them away and hide them behind the liquidizer. When we have a tin of condensed milk we always have a quick sneaky spoonful but dad always sticks his head through the hatch and catches us.

Alison Age 10

My father is a man of the house, my father can tell you to do this and do that.
'Stephen, come down here at once."
See what I mean? The father of the house must have what he wants.
My dad says "Come here, go there," I think he is driving me pottey or up the wall.
Sometimes.

Stephen Age 11

If dads are the generals of the house, big brothers and sister are the sargeant-majors.

Timothy Robinson Age 12

Dads always want to be correct. Maybe yours isn't, but mine is!

Gordon

Stephen

'Pull your socks up, make your bed,
Tuck your shirt in, get a haircut,
Tidy your room, brush the dog,
Do your tie up, clean your teeth,
Take those jeans off, they're filthy,
What did you say to me then?

'Shut the blinds, wash the car,
Take the dog out, clean your shoes,
Go and get the coal, turn that row off,
A tidy room means a tidy mind,
All you do is laze around,
What was that I heard you say?

'Turn the light off after you leave a room,
Put your clothes away, mow the lawns,
Fix that window, prune the grape vine,
The same leopard has the same spots,
Don't argue, and toe the line,
Don't talk to me in that insolent manner!'

Andrew Age 14

Pocket money

Dads are like moving banks.

John Age 11

I don't get much pocket money I think there should be a law that you give your child £2.50 a week or else they have to go to jail.

Debbie

My father is a sport fanatic, especially for football. In the evening if his team has lost he is gloomy and down-hearted. When it's a win he's glowing with excitement; now is the time to ask for the extra ten pence pocket money.

Fiona Age 13

My dad is a cop but even so my dad still pinches money out of my mum's purse.

Mandy

When Dad comes home from work he likes me to cuddle him and I do, especially on pocket money days.

Karen Age 10

My dad is extremely stingy with his precious money and keeps it in a specially built vault under our house. The day I am given my pocket money on time will be a day for Celebrations.

Guy Age 12

Dads are there not to give you pocket money but to help you, love you and to care for you.

David Harvey

When my dad has a few drinks
He staggers up the path
He gives me a fiver
And when he is sober
He says "Where's my fiver?"

Gareth

54

Lincoln Age 10

I get 60p pocket money a week. How am I supposed to live on that with the present rate of inflation?

Stephen Munday

Judith Gracie Age 10

Growing pains

My dad is always shouting at me and not my little
sisster wich ido-not think is fair. My little sisster
dosent seem to think what i think she seems to think it
is fair of course LITTLE SISSTERS are awful.

John Age 9

Daddies are always on at you. Daddy says "Go to
bed at 8 o/Clock" when I don't go 'til 8.15. And insists
prep is done properly and is always reminding about
being polite.
OH PARENTS.

Rebecca Age 10

Another thing I find boring is when I arrive
home and Dad asks me if I am doing well at school. As
if I knew the answer to the question.

Richard Age 12

Dads are always looking for things to tell you off
for, like to stand up when someone older than you
comes in; I think it's just a waste of time.

John Age 10

My dad is always on to us about being rude (as
though he is such an angel.) Yet every day when we're
eating, (especially when we have guests) he comes up
with rude subjects (which I won't mention). My dad is
always on to me about swearing. BUT! I have heard
him swear five times in the last few days. When he is
driving the car, for some mysterious reason he keeps
on picking his nose. Yet he is always on to us about
these things. If I told you some of the things he did
when he was a boy I could go on forever, so I'd better
stop now.

Stephen

My father at lunch time says *"Stop making that
noise"* making more noise than anyone else.

Patricia Age 9

Beware of Dads!
Dads are second Mums.
If you upset Mum you have got dad to deal with,
Dads are nice to have around,
When you want new clothes.

Dad has 'tidy up' sessions at the
most unexpected times
Dad has the loudest voice,
Beware of dad!!

Dad means shaving cream,
Musk after shave,
Match of the day,
Saturday afternoon naps,
Dad means . . . dad.

Patricia Age 13

Up to Bed. Why?
Get in the Bath. Why?
Because you're dirty
Go and put the milk on Bobby
Supper's ready. What is it?
Come and see. Oh Yum, Yum.
Don't pick.
Can I watch Cannon? No!

Duncan Age 9

*Simon
Perrin
Age 7*

My dad tells me to throw away odd things to
make more space which he immediately fills with
antiques.

Andrew Age 12

If a father asks his son to bring him the slippers,
he will obey straightaway; but if a son kindly requires
his father to do the same, the slippers will be thrown
upon his head.

Alberto Age 14

Soft on the inside

Daddy likes swimming, reading making things and Mommy and I. My daddy has a funny habit of saying checkes little madam. My daddy is nice on the outsides, and on the insides.

Siobhan

My daddy is like plasticine, he is all hard and grotty, but when we do something like sweep the floor he goes all soft and smiley.

Gemma Age 11

I like my dad because when he tells me off which is very unusual he says it in a soft deep voice and I don't feel hurt at all.

Tracy Sims Age 9

Fathers are gumpy people but are good at heart. Their are kind in a different way to mothers.

Amanda Age 10

Most of all Mum gives us love and Dad does as well in a rougher attitude.

David Benge Age 12

The trouble with my dad is that he is ether mad or soft and nice.

Guy

My dad is quite nice if you approach him okay.

Fiona

In the eighteenth century a father was hard on the outside and inside. By the twenties he was hard outside but soft inside. Nowadays he is soft both outside and inside.

Mark Wickham-Jones Age 13

A father is the big hefty head of the house, the big man outwardly whose interior is usually very soft.

Stephen Thomas Age 15

A father is a man that moves around the home with a big stick in one hand and love in the other.

Rayna Age 12

Although their faces may look strict,
And they may get in a rage,
We don't forget and must agree,
Their great for all their age!

Susan Age 11

My father is an angry fellow.
He roars his head off sometimes.
But inside him I think he is not so bad.

James Age 10

My dad is the biggest teaser around.
But his kindness
Changes everything.

Jane Livermore Age 11

Nicholas Age 8

Nothing but love

Parenthood is serious business.

Aysegul Corekci Age 15

A man becomes a father only when his wife gives birth to a child. Till then he is only an ordinary man. When a man becomes a father he becomes the most responsible man on the earth.

Sandeep Sampat Age 15

My father is gay but he sometimes sits on his chair looking sad and would not part from us for all the riches in the world.

Judy S Garcia Age 9

When we get a big job we must not forget them because when we were small they did not forget us. When they are old and sick we must not leave them as strangers.

Michael M Rambert Age 11

Big, strong, athletic
Shrewd, just, understanding
Loving, fun, dependable
Always busy with business.

Evan Green

Robert Jones Age 8

Euan Leckie Age 7

Some dads give them everything except love, some give them nothing but love.

Aysegul Corekci Age 15

I call him a real dad

My dad is a dad anybody could want. He'll do anything. Every Sunday morning my dad takes me to Hackney Marshes to watch football and to play. After that when we come home we might go out to relatives or for a ride.

He always makes sure that I get to school early. When I come home I might go to the shop with him and to keep him company I cut the chips, I flour the fish too. He always lets me stay up late. On our birthdays he always gets what I want. He lets me go on outings that the school has had. One day I was coming to school when I just remembered my outing money so I rung him up and told him about it so he told me to wait at the station so he could give it to me. He helps me do any-thing. I was making a model for school one day not propely when dad came home he turned it into a masterpiece he told me to get up early the next day and paint it when I came down the next morning I saw that he had put an undercoat of paint so when I paint with water colours I won't find it difficult. He never breaks a promise. I ask him if I could have my watch fixed for Christmas instead of having anything new. I call him a real dad.

Steven Piponides

My father is a man of integrity. He is loyal to both his family and country. He maintains good discipline in our family and we all respect him very much. If all fathers were like my father what a wonderful world this would be.

Joan Gunter Age 15

If my father promises something to me he would never break it.

Vazita Fadakas

A tribute to my father

We do not have any choice when it comes to dads, we are lucky or unlucky, and I am one of the lucky ones.

My dad is in his forties, about five feet seven, going a bit bald on top. He is always saying he is the best looking man in Bickley, joking of course, he is always joking. Still my mum thinks he is handsome.

There are lots of things I like about my dad, I can never remember him saying nasty things about anyone, he will not let you feel sorry for yourself. If I were to complain about having to walk a long way, and that my legs were hurting, he would say a man with no legs would love to say that. Not many of us always think of someone worse off than ourselves but my dad does.

Everyone has a weakness and my dad's is chocolate. My mum says it's not fair, eating chocolate like dad does, and still staying nice and slim. He is always ready for a game of any sort.

Most of all he is kind, and gentle. We all love him very much. I know that it is said that everyone has faults. If my dad has any they are so few they don't seem to show.

Susan Lewis Age 11

God keep our fathers as nice as they have always been.

Jane Moppel Age 12

Julia Watch

Is there a birthday coming up soon?

If you enjoyed *To Dad,* why not order another in the series? The books make lovely birthday and Christmas gifts.

To Mum, £2.25
'If I threw a rock at my mother she'd still love me.'
A thoughtful, joyful gift.

Happy Families, £2.25
"A family is a mother and father to love, and a brother or sister to fight with." A lovely gift for any member of the family.

Grandmas & Grandpas, £2.25
'A grandma is old on the outside and young on the inside.'

What is a husband? £2.50
7,500 real wives answered that question and the best quotes are here. Pithy, beautiful, rude, hilarious, sad and romantic.

Shopping by Post, £4.50 (£1.95 paperback)
Whether you want a needle-threader or a folding bicycle by post, this book tells you which firm to write to.

See Britain at Work, £4.95
The first guidebook of its kind. 300 glassworks, potteries, power stations, car plants and small craft industries you can visit.

Order any of these books through your local bookshop — or you can get them by sending a cheque or postal order to Exley Publications, 63 Kingsfield Road, Watford WD1 4PP.